Ancient China

LOUISE SPILSBURY

raintree
a Capstone company — publishers for children

Raintree is an imprint of Capstone Global Library Limited, a company incorporated in England and Wales having its registered office at 264 Banbury Road, Oxford, OX2 7DY – Registered company number: 6695582

www.raintree.co.uk
myorders@raintree.co.uk

Original illustrations © Capstone Global Library Limited 2020
Originated by Capstone Global Library Ltd
Printed and bound in India

ISBN 978 1 4747 7772 8 (hardback)
ISBN 978 1 4747 7781 0 (paperback)

British Library Cataloguing in Publication Data
A full catalogue record for this book is available from the British Library.

Acknowledgements
We would like to thank the following for permission to reproduce photographs: Cover: Shutterstock: Hung Chung Chih: top; Zhu Difen: bottom; Inside: Flickr: Tak.wing CC BY-SA 2.0: p .25; Shutterstock: Beibaoke: pp. 15r, 16–17; Mark Brandon: pp. 14–15; Enzo Bro: p. 26; Chinahbzyg: p. 41b; DnDavis: pp. 30–31; Javarman: p. 39br; Jiraphoto: pp. 40–41; Lapas77: p. 31br; Marzolino: pp. 32–33; Raymoe81: p. 18; Robbihafzan: p. 7r; Rongyiquan: pp. 8–9; Deborah Lee Rossiter: p. 29b; Superjoseph: p. 10; Thanannopthanoch Thongmam: p. 21b; Wikimedia Commons: pp. 9r, 11, 22, 36; Acot: pp. 6–7; Chez Cåsver (Xuan Che): p. 27; Daderot: pp. 19, 20–21, 24, 33br, 44–45, 45r; Su Hanchen: p. 17t; Le Bas, Aliamet, Prevot, Saint-Aubin, Masquelier, Choffard, and Launay: pp. 4–5; Mingdynastyavenger: pp. 12–13; Peabody Essex Museum: pp. 28–29; PericlesofAthens: pp. 38–39; Sailko: p. 23; Daniel Schwen: p. 35b; Snowyowls: p. 13r; Wellcome Collection: pp. 1, 5r, 42–43, 43br.

Every effort has been made to contact copyright holders of material reproduced in this book. Any omissions will be rectified in subsequent printings if notice is given to the publisher.

All the internet addresses (URLs) given in this book were valid at the time of going to press. However, due to the dynamic nature of the internet, some addresses may have changed, or sites may have changed or ceased to exist since publication. While the author and publisher regret any inconvenience this may cause readers, no responsibility for any such changes can be accepted by either the author or the publisher.

Contents

Chapter 1 Deadly dynasties 4

Weapons of destruction 6

The mighty Qin 8

Chapter 2 Evil emperors 10

Sinister spies 12

Murderous mother 14

Chapter 3 Gruesome graves 16

Terrible tombs 18

Suits of death 20

Chapter 4 Angry ancestors 22

Human sacrifice 24

Secrets in the bones........................ 26

Chapter 5 Worked to death 28

A job to die for! 30

Suffering slaves 32

Chapter 6 Horrible habits 34

Macabre make-up 36

Disgusting dinners 38

Terrible toilets................................ 40

Nasty medicines.............................. 42

A bloody end.................................. 44

Glossary 46

Find out more 47

Index.. 48

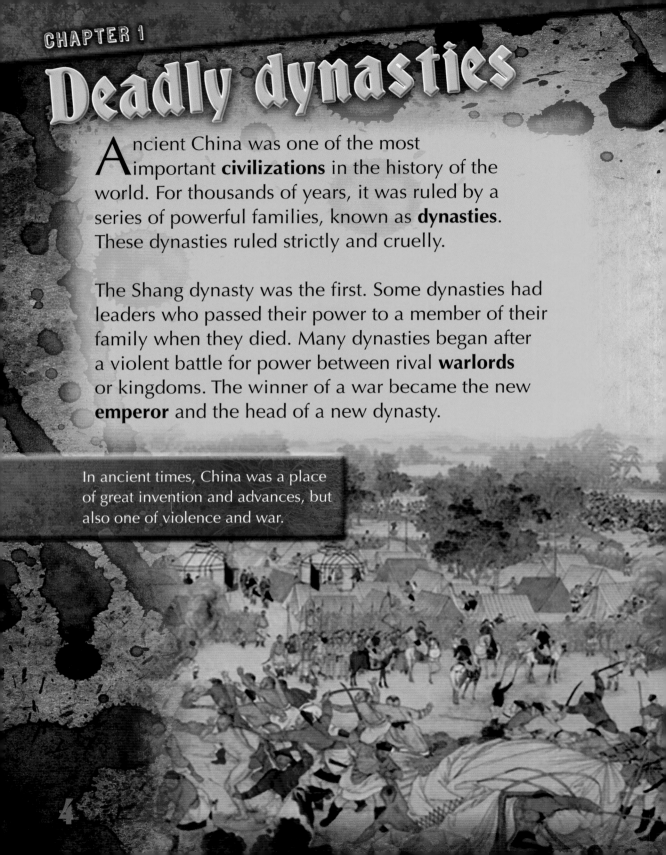

CHAPTER 1

Deadly dynasties

Ancient China was one of the most important **civilizations** in the history of the world. For thousands of years, it was ruled by a series of powerful families, known as **dynasties**. These dynasties ruled strictly and cruelly.

The Shang dynasty was the first. Some dynasties had leaders who passed their power to a member of their family when they died. Many dynasties began after a violent battle for power between rival **warlords** or kingdoms. The winner of a war became the new **emperor** and the head of a new dynasty.

In ancient times, China was a place of great invention and advances, but also one of violence and war.

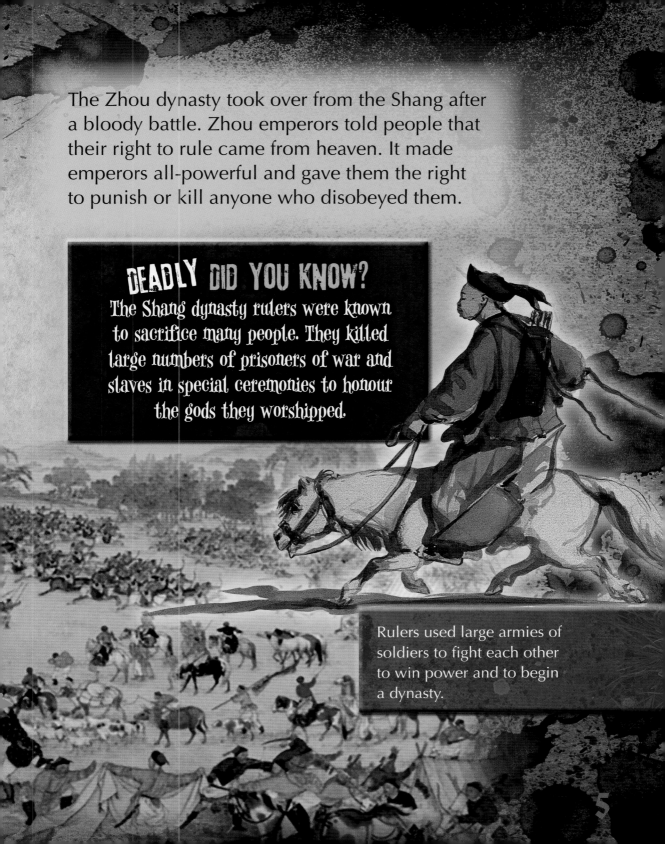

The Zhou dynasty took over from the Shang after a bloody battle. Zhou emperors told people that their right to rule came from heaven. It made emperors all-powerful and gave them the right to punish or kill anyone who disobeyed them.

DEADLY DID YOU KNOW?

The Shang dynasty rulers were known to sacrifice many people. They killed large numbers of prisoners of war and slaves in special ceremonies to honour the gods they worshipped.

Rulers used large armies of soldiers to fight each other to win power and to begin a dynasty.

Weapons of destruction

The rulers of China's deadly dynasties gained and kept their power using large, bloodthirsty armies that were equipped with lethal weapons.

Chariots proved to be a powerful weapon of war. Horse-drawn chariots allowed warriors to chase enemies across the wide, open spaces of ancient China. They could kill opponents from their chariots and take large areas of land under their control.

These are the remains of a Shang warrior's chariot and horses, which were found in a grave.

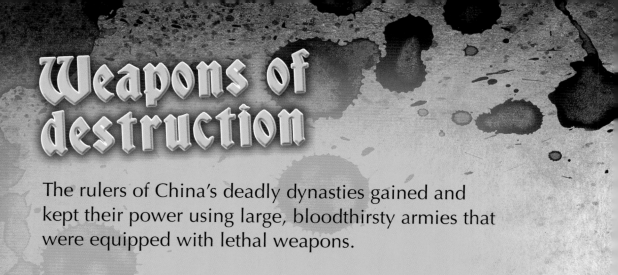

Chinese warriors fired arrows from large bows and hurled long spears with steel tips at enemies from a distance. They launched ten bolts every fifteen seconds from their crossbows. In closer combat, they attacked with **bronze** daggers, battle axes and doubled-edged swords.

KILLER FACT!

Ancient Chinese warriors attached special devices to kites. The devices made low, moaning sounds and high-pitched wails in the wind. Enemies hearing these sounds, coming from something they were unable to see clearly, thought that the gods were angry with them and ran away.

Chinese warriors also used kites to send messages to each other during a large battle.

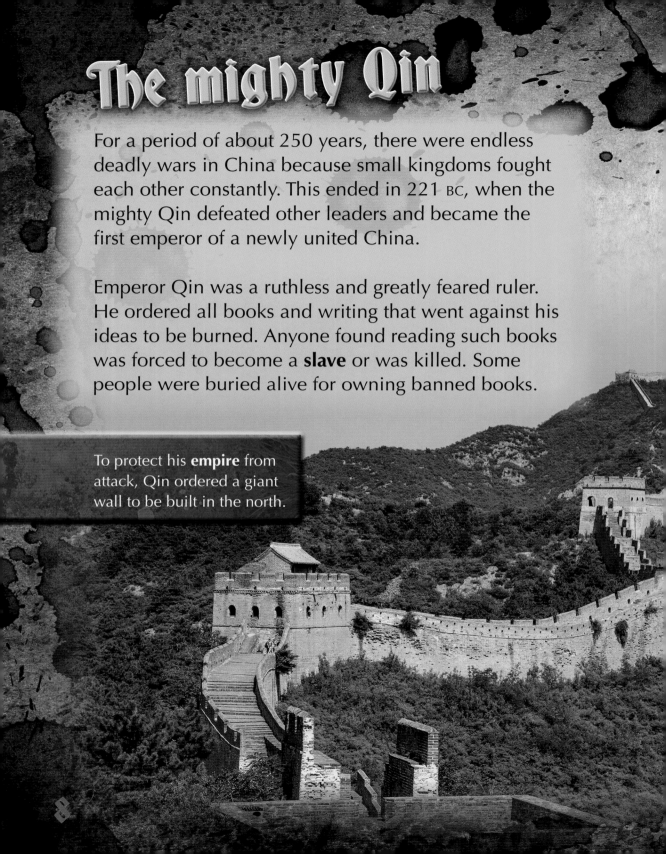

The mighty Qin

For a period of about 250 years, there were endless deadly wars in China because small kingdoms fought each other constantly. This ended in 221 BC, when the mighty Qin defeated other leaders and became the first emperor of a newly united China.

Emperor Qin was a ruthless and greatly feared ruler. He ordered all books and writing that went against his ideas to be burned. Anyone found reading such books was forced to become a **slave** or was killed. Some people were buried alive for owning banned books.

To protect his **empire** from attack, Qin ordered a giant wall to be built in the north.

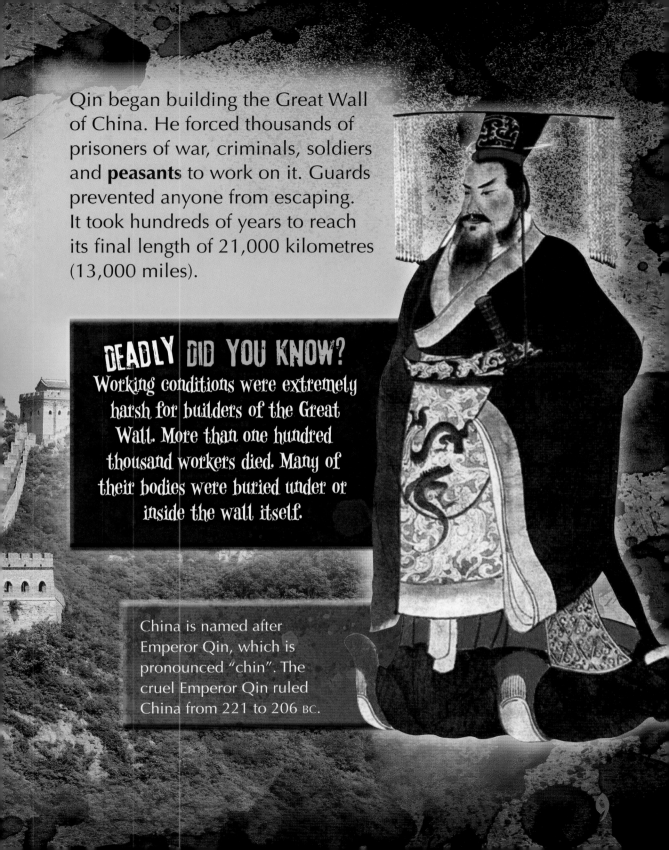

Qin began building the Great Wall of China. He forced thousands of prisoners of war, criminals, soldiers and **peasants** to work on it. Guards prevented anyone from escaping. It took hundreds of years to reach its final length of 21,000 kilometres (13,000 miles).

DEADLY DID YOU KNOW?

Working conditions were extremely harsh for builders of the Great Wall. More than one hundred thousand workers died. Many of their bodies were buried under or inside the wall itself.

China is named after Emperor Qin, which is pronounced "chin". The cruel Emperor Qin ruled China from 221 to 206 BC.

CHAPTER 2

Evil emperors

Qin was just the first in a long line of evil emperors. Emperor Yongle ruled from 1402 to 1424. He became known for a type of torture called "death by a thousand cuts".

Death by a thousand cuts was carried out by cutting off pieces of a victim's flesh over a long period of time. This meant that the person suffered agonizing pain before he or she died.

Emperor Yongle's palace complex had more than nine thousand rooms.

Yongle wanted to own the largest palace complex ever known. More than one million workers were forced to drag giant slabs of marble many kilometres across ice from the north to build the Forbidden City. If a stone was damaged, the worker who delivered it could be punished with death by a thousand cuts.

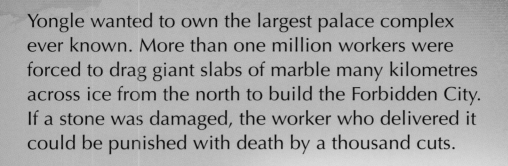

DEADLY DID YOU KNOW?

Yongle insisted that people kowtow to him. This is kneeling three times and tapping the forehead against the ground nine times. Anyone who forgot to do this might also have suffered death by a thousand cuts.

Some Chinese emperors used their power for good, but many, such as Yongle, used it to satisfy their own greed.

Sinister spies

Another emperor, Hongwu, set up the dreaded Jinyi Wei as his personal bodyguards. Later, they were used as a secret police to crush any opposition. The Jinyi Wei were used to watch over officials and root out **rebels**, but these spies were often **corrupt**.

Jinyi Wei guards could decide someone was guilty, even if it was a lie. They often demanded money as a bribe to let someone go. Anyone who refused to pay the bribe was put in prison and tortured to death.

Hongwu ordered some people to be killed by **flaying**. Their skin was cut away from their body while they were still alive. The flesh was nailed to a wall as a warning to others not to disobey the horrible Emperor Hongwu.

The Jinyi Wei were the most feared men in Hongwu's empire.

錦衣衛指揮使馬順

KILLER FACT!

Jinyi Wei guards wore a distinctive dragon on their uniform, an ivory tablet on their chest and carried a special and deadly blade. Their tablet gave them the power to arrest, question and torture anyone they chose.

When people saw a guard wearing an ivory tablet such as this they knew he was a Jinyi Wei and they were terrified.

Murderous mother

Empress Wu is famous for being a ruthless rule-breaker who let no one stand in the way of her rise to power.

Wu is accused of killing her own week-old daughter and blaming the baby's death on Wang, the emperor's favourite wife. The emperor believed Wu's story and imprisoned Wang in a distant part of the palace. This made Wu the favourite. After the emperor died, Wu become empress.

Wu was the only female empress in ancient China's history. She held onto power by keeping her government terrified of what she might do if they crossed her.

A giant statue of Buddha in the Longmen Grottoes in China is believed to have been modelled on the face of Empress Wu.

Empress Wu got rid of any officials who opposed her rule while she was empress. She fired them, banished them from the kingdom or had them executed.

This statue of Wu is in Huangze Temple, the only one in China that honours the empress.

CHAPTER 3

Gruesome graves

The ancient Chinese believed in an **afterlife**, so they buried items in people's graves to go with them in their next life. This included pots, jewels and human **sacrifices**.

Fu Hao was the most powerful woman in the Shang dynasty. She was a military leader and led the army in great and successful battles against enemies. She was also a priest who performed ceremonies and sacrifices.

Fu Hao's grave contains a lot of weapons, jewellery and shells, which the ancient Chinese used as a form of money. There were also sixteen unfortunate servants who were killed and buried with her, so that they could serve her in the afterlife.

Fu Hao's tomb is the only tomb of a member of the Shang royal family to have been found unlooted.

KILLER FACT!

Six dogs were also sacrificed and buried alongside Fu Hao in her gruesome grave. Dog sacrifices were made when tombs were completed. Dogs were often buried to ward off evil spirits or bad luck.

In ancient China, dogs were eaten as food, used for guarding, herding and hunting, and they were sacrificed to please the gods.

Terrible tombs

China's early emperors wanted to live forever. They sent officials out on a search across China for potions and herbs that might give them the **immortality** they desired. For example, Emperor Qin swallowed **mercury** because he thought it could prolong his life. But mercury is deadly poisonous. Qin died on a tour of his empire and officials sneaked him back to the palace with dried fish to disguise the smell of his decaying flesh.

The discovery of some terrible tombs shows that emperors also tried other, more dreadful methods to help them cheat death. At one site **archaeologists** discovered the remains of 113 young children, some as young as two years old. It is believed they were all sacrificed by an emperor seeking eternal life.

By the time Emperor Qin was buried, his body must have been badly decayed.

KILLER FACT!

The bodies of the 113 children had been cut up after they were sacrificed. The children's skulls and feet were buried separately, arranged in two small urns made of pottery. The main body parts were buried in a larger urn. Small holes were drilled in the side of the clay coating to allow the soul to come and go freely.

Pots, called burial urns, similar to this one were used to bury parts of the sacrificed children.

Suits of death

Emperors and other important members of royal families were not only buried with objects they would need when they joined the gods in the afterlife, but some were also covered head to toe in suits made from jade before being buried. Jade is a precious green stone.

The ancient Chinese believed that jade had magical powers. Jade suits contained about two thousand separate plates of jade. The plates were sewn together around a **corpse** with gold, silver or bronze wire, depending on how important the dead person was.

Royals and **nobles** started planning their burials long before they died because it could take up to ten years to make a jade suit. The suits encased their bodies and were shaped to look like a protective suit of armour.

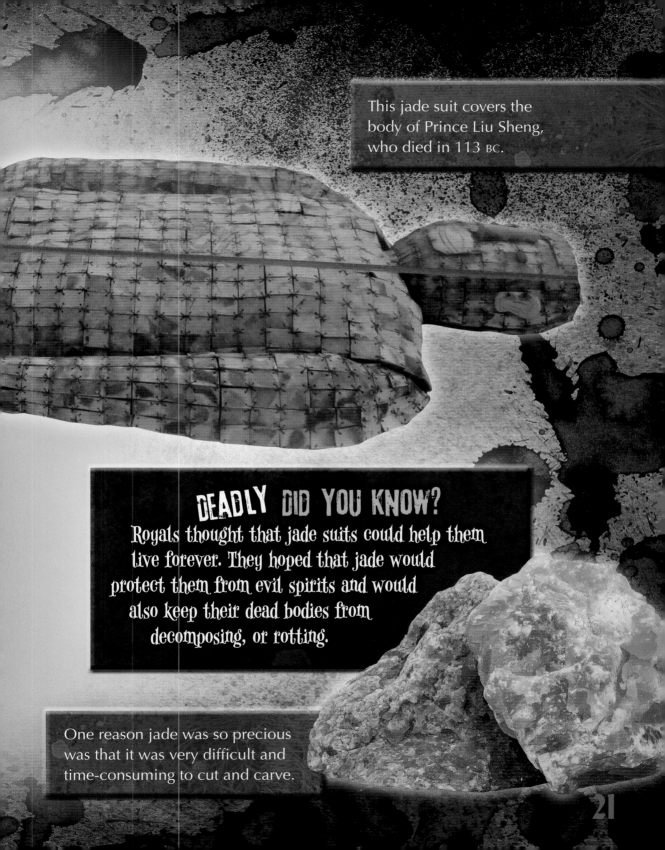

This jade suit covers the body of Prince Liu Sheng, who died in 113 BC.

DEADLY DID YOU KNOW?

Royals thought that jade suits could help them live forever. They hoped that jade would protect them from evil spirits and would also keep their dead bodies from decomposing, or rotting.

One reason jade was so precious was that it was very difficult and time-consuming to cut and carve.

CHAPTER 4

Angry ancestors

The ancient Chinese believed there were many different gods who had power over different parts of their lives. The only way to contact them was through their **ancestors**.

People carried out **rituals** to honour their ancestors and took good care of their graves. They believed that this kept the ancestors happy so they would ask the gods to bring good luck. If people neglected a dead relative, the ancestor could become a "hungry ghost". They could be dangerous and allow terrible things to happen.

This table is filled with offerings to the dead ancestors whose images are hung around the walls of the room.

To show respect to their ancestors, people left **offerings** of food and wine at grave sites and shrines. These gifts were carried in beautiful containers called *ding*. The food and wine were meant to help the ancestors survive during the afterlife.

During the Shang dynasty, people also sacrificed animals to honour their ancestors. Animals such as sheep and pigs were sacrificed in large numbers at ritual ceremonies.

DEADLY DID YOU KNOW?
Ding were elaborate pots made from bronze. The ancient Chinese hoped the offerings inside the *ding* would show honour and respect to the ancestors.

A three-legged bronze *ding* such as this would have been used to make ritual offerings of food and drink to ancestors.

Human sacrifice

During the Shang dynasty, many human sacrifices were made. Large numbers of people were cruelly murdered in honour of kings and sometimes queens, and to worship or contact the gods.

To worship male ancestors such as emperors, the Shang priests chose mostly male victims for sacrifice. The young men were aged between fifteen and thirty-five and came from outside **tribes**. By sacrificing these victims to the ancestors, Shang people hoped to avoid bad luck.

The skeletons of unfortunate victims of cruel sacrifices sometimes reveal the ways in which they were killed.

Different methods were used in ritual sacrifices. Victims were **beheaded**, cut in half, beaten or bled to death, chopped into pieces, buried alive, drowned or boiled. Burning sacrifices was seen as a way to send the dead, in the form of smoke, up to heaven.

KILLER FACT!

The most common method of sacrifice for a male victim during the Shang dynasty was cutting off his head using a dagger or a sacrificial knife. Then the head was offered to the spirits.

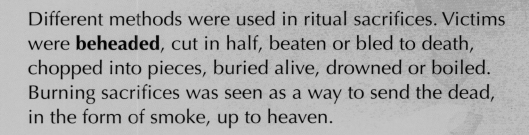

Beheading people from different tribes using a sacrificial knife was also a way to scare off outsiders.

Secrets in the bones

Some rulers used special oracle bones to find out when would be the best day to offer sacrifices to their ancestors or gods. Oracle bones were usually made from the shoulder blade of an ox. Bones from other animals, such as horses, pigs and deer, were also used, as well as tortoise shells.

The bone was sawn to shape and shallow pits were drilled on one side. A question was written on it in red ink. Hot metal spikes put into the hollow pits caused the bones to crack. If the bone cracked on one side, the answer to the question was "yes". If it cracked on the other, the answer was "no".

A king's name, the date, the priest's name, the answer and the number of cracks were all recorded on an oracle bone.

DEADLY DID YOU KNOW?

Ancient Chinese rulers asked oracle bones things such as when was the best time to fight a battle and the correct way to perform certain rituals. The oracle bones even told priests how a sacrificial victim should die. So a victim could be beheaded or drowned, depending on the way the oracle bone cracked.

Oracle bones were often buried alongside dead rulers in a pit.

27

CHAPTER 5

Worked to death

While emperors and the royal family lived in luxury and planned their detailed burials, life was hard for ordinary Chinese people. Many of them were worked to death.

Silk was the most precious fabric in all of ancient China. Many people outside the kingdom of China wanted to buy it and they were willing to pay a very high price for this beautiful cloth. The emperors of China kept how silk was made a closely guarded secret.

Silk was used to make the most beautiful robes for Chinese rulers.

Silk was made using the larvae (caterpillars) of silk moths. The larvae spun silk thread cocoons around themselves when they were ready to transform into moths. Workers steamed the cocoons to kill the moth growing inside, and then removed the threads and spun them together to make silk.

KILLER FACT!

There was a law to stop the workers who made the silk from ever revealing how it was made. If a worker was caught stealing silk moth eggs or cocoons, or telling someone how the silk was made, he or she was tortured to death.

Many thousands of silk moth caterpillars were killed to make silk in ancient China.

A job to die for!

Many ordinary people worked on palaces and other huge building projects for the power-hungry emperors. It took a hardworking team of around 700,000 workers more than forty years to build a vast army made from a type of clay, called terracotta, for Emperor Qin. It was the last job they would ever do.

The eight thousand life-size soldiers are buried near Emperor Qin's tomb. They were made to protect him in the afterlife.

As well as soldiers, there are also clay horses and chariots in the incredible Terracotta Army, which was not discovered until 1974.

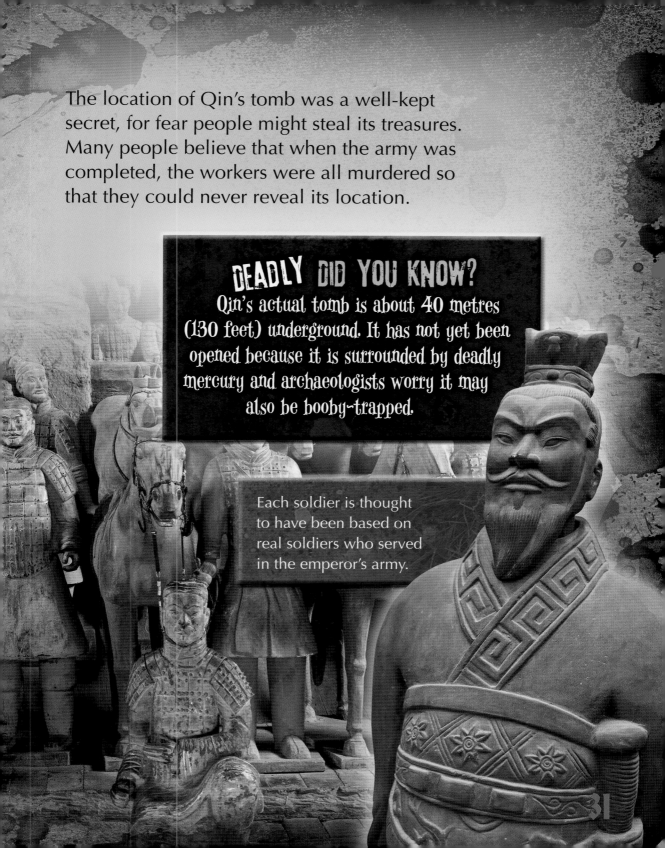

The location of Qin's tomb was a well-kept secret, for fear people might steal its treasures. Many people believe that when the army was completed, the workers were all murdered so that they could never reveal its location.

DEADLY DID YOU KNOW?

Qin's actual tomb is about 40 metres (130 feet) underground. It has not yet been opened because it is surrounded by deadly mercury and archaeologists worry it may also be booby-trapped.

Each soldier is thought to have been based on real soldiers who served in the emperor's army.

Suffering slaves

The lives of the slaves were the hardest of all and they were given the most horrible jobs. Slaves had to do any job they were told to, without any payment. They had to work hard for their masters and were treated with great cruelty.

Some people were forced to become slaves if their relative was a criminal condemned to death. When an emperor's army defeated an enemy, the army also captured prisoners who were then made into slaves.

Slaves built palaces, dug tombs, constructed roads and bridges, cut trees for timber and worked down mines digging out metals such as copper. They sweated by large fires to make tools and over pans of boiling seawater to get salt.

Slaves carried royals and nobles from place to place in a large box called a *palanquin*.

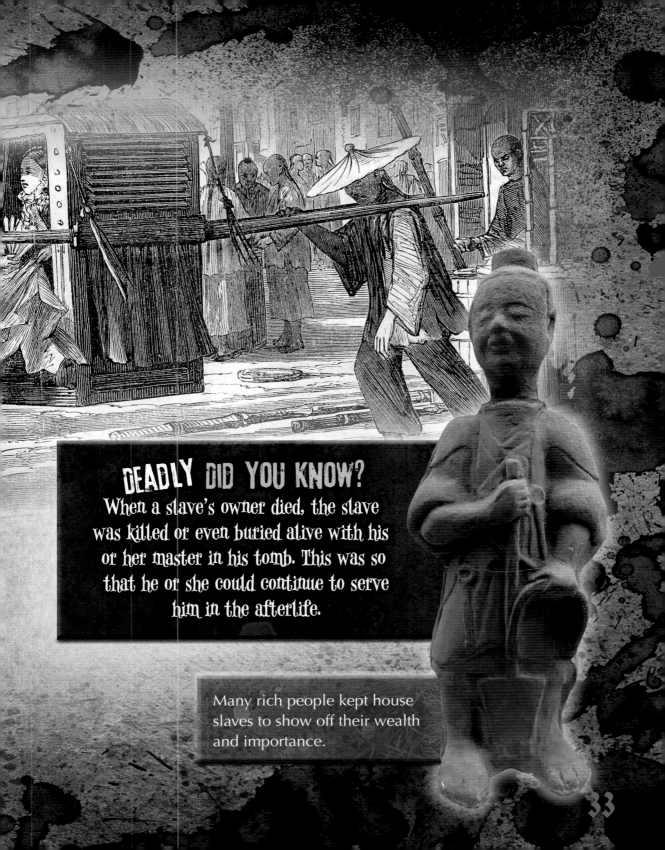

DEADLY DID YOU KNOW?

When a slave's owner died, the slave was killed or even buried alive with his or her master in his tomb. This was so that he or she could continue to serve him in the afterlife.

Many rich people kept house slaves to show off their wealth and importance.

CHAPTER 6

Horrible habits

The ancient Chinese had many horrible habits. These range from wearing foot bindings and macabre make-up to eating awful meals.

The ancient Chinese thought tiny feet were beautiful. Tiny feet also ensured young girls sat still while they helped make goods such as cloth, mats and fishing nets for families to sell.

To make sure a girl's feet were kept tiny, at a young age the toes on her feet were broken and folded under her feet. The foot arches were bent double and were strapped tightly and painfully into place by a long silk strip.

Girls with bound feet were forced to walk and play to speed up the breaking of their arches.

KILLER FACT!

Once bound, over the next two years, the straps were only briefly removed to clean blood and pus, and to cut away excess flesh. After that, the feet were crushed permanently together and were tiny.

Shoes worn by girls with bound feet were about the length of a mobile phone and not much wider.

Macabre make-up

In ancient China, women went to great lengths to make themselves look beautiful. Women had little power, so one reason they wore make-up was to attract a husband. Their tiny feet and silk robes also showed off their family's wealth and importance.

The ingredients used in make-up were truly horrible. Women in ancient China coloured their lips with a paste made from the leaves of red and blue flowering plants mixed with oil or fat from cows and pigs. They decorated their cheeks and forehead by gluing on fish scales, bird feathers and dragonfly wings.

In ancient China, white skin, red cheeks and large red lips were fashionable.

Women shaved their eyebrows and painted new ones on using soot from burned willow branches. To make the face look whiter, some women used a mixture of vinegar and lead. Unfortunately, over time the lead would eat away the skin, causing painful scars.

DEADLY DID YOU KNOW?
To stick flower petals and other decorative items to their cheeks, women in ancient China often used fish guts as a strange, and probably very smelly, sort of glue.

A make-up box could have held a mirror, rouge for cheeks and lipstick.

Disgusting dinners

In ancient China, most people ate quite a healthy diet with a lot of rice and vegetables. But some of the dishes on the menu at a feast were disgusting.

One speciality was urine eggs. These were just as you would imagine from the name. Eggs were boiled for an entire day in the urine of boys under the age of ten. The ancient Chinese thought these eggs were very good for their health.

Bears' paws, camels' humps, apes' lips rhinoceroses' tails and sharks' fins were considered **delicacies** at feasts and festivals.

Some feasts lasted three days or more and included more than 320 different dishes.

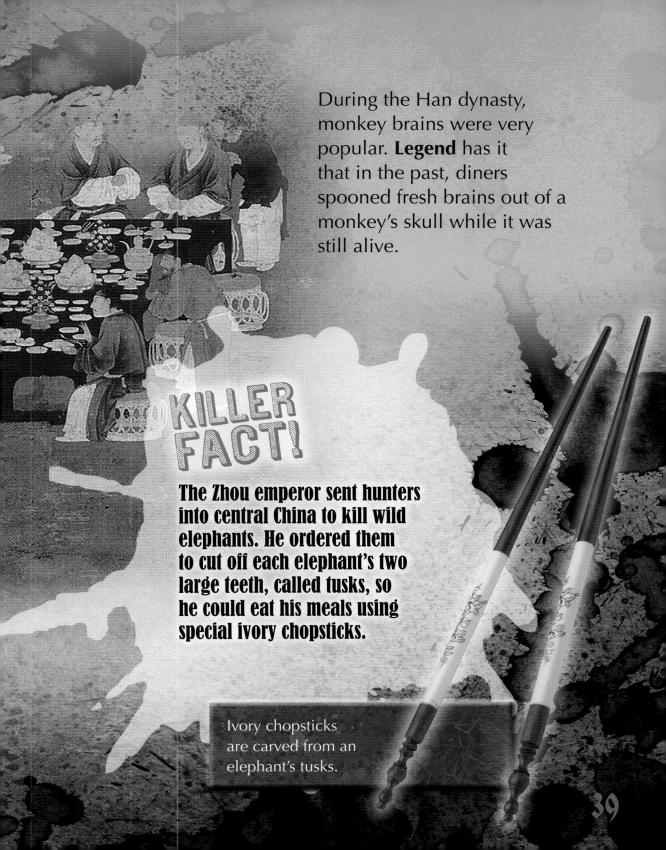

During the Han dynasty, monkey brains were very popular. **Legend** has it that in the past, diners spooned fresh brains out of a monkey's skull while it was still alive.

KILLER FACT!

The Zhou emperor sent hunters into central China to kill wild elephants. He ordered them to cut off each elephant's two large teeth, called tusks, so he could eat his meals using special ivory chopsticks.

Ivory chopsticks are carved from an elephant's tusks.

Terrible toilets

Ancient Chinese farmers were among the first recyclers. They never threw anything away that could be useful. They even made use of their toilet waste.

In early China, human **faeces** were collected from public toilets and sold to farmers. The farmers spread this human waste, known as "night-soil" on their fields to act as cheap fertilizer. Collecting faeces was such a good way to earn money in ancient China that there was even a saying about it: "treasure night-soil as if it were gold".

Spreading human waste onto terraces to help rice grow must have been a horrible, smelly job.

Some farmers in ancient China built a special type of outbuilding above the pen where they kept their pigs. They built a room over the pen that they used as a toilet so that their faeces would fall directly into the pigs' trough below. For the pigs in the pen beneath them, this was their dinner.

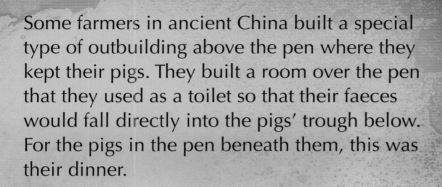

DEADLY DID YOU KNOW?

Toilet paper was one of ancient China's many great inventions, but only the emperors were allowed to use it. Some other people wiped themselves clean with a bamboo stick that had a strip of fabric wound around it. They used this once and threw it away.

Some ancient Chinese people collected urine in ceramic pots and washed their armpits with it.

41

Nasty medicines

The ancient Chinese used a variety of strange medicines but some of them really worked. During the early dynasties, people thought illnesses were caused by evil spirits. They chanted spells and ate crushed **fossils**, which they thought were dragon bones, to be cured.

To cure **diarrhoea**, ancient Chinese doctors recommended eating a yellow soup. It smelled and tasted awful because it contained faeces from a healthy person, but it worked.

Acupuncture is an ancient Chinese treatment that involves sticking needles into certain points of the body. Like many other Chinese inventions and discoveries, acupuncture works and is still used to stop pain and prevent illness all over the world today.

This picture shows the acupuncture points (where to stick the needles) for the front of the head.

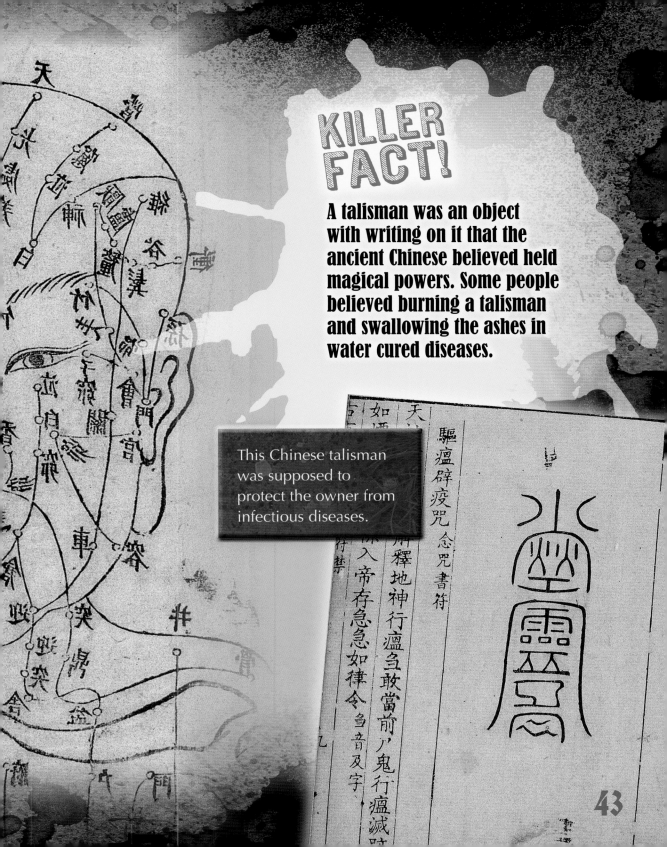

KILLER FACT!

A talisman was an object with writing on it that the ancient Chinese believed held magical powers. Some people believed burning a talisman and swallowing the ashes in water cured diseases.

This Chinese talisman was supposed to protect the owner from infectious diseases.

A bloody end

The last ancient Chinese dynasty was the Han dynasty. The Han dynasty ended in AD 220. Many people believe that the era of Chinese dynasties ended much as it had begun, in blood and violence.

The final years of the Han dynasty were plagued with natural disasters and one Han emperor after another died young or without an **heir**. Ordinary people started to think that these events were signs that the gods were unhappy with their leaders.

Fights for control broke out between members of the ruling families, and peasants started to rebel against their leaders. Then a warlord called Dong Zhou took control of the country. By 220, the last emperor was gone and the Han dynasty was over.

By the Han dynasty, people were tired of watching emperors and the rich living in luxury and riding around in chariots.

DEADLY DID YOU KNOW?

After AD 220, China was ripped apart by deadly wars between different regions. It was hundreds of years before China was a united country again.

This is a model of a Han warrior. These soldiers were unable to defeat the warlords who finally overran the ancient Chinese Empire.

Glossary

afterlife life after death. Some people believe that after we die we live in another world.

ancestors relatives who have died

archaeologists people who study objects to learn about how people lived in the past

beheaded killed by cutting off the head

bronze metal made from a mixture of melted metals

civilizations settled communities in which people live together and use systems, such as writing, to communicate

corpse dead body

corrupt doing things that are dishonest or illegal in order to make money or to gain or keep power

delicacies food that is rare or luxurious

diarrhoea condition that involves unusually frequent and liquid bowel movements

dynasties when one family rules a country for a long time, because after a leader dies their eldest son takes over

emperor male leader or ruler of an empire

empire large area of land or group of countries ruled over by one leader

faeces digestive waste

flaying stripping off the skin

fossils remains of dead plants and animals from millions of years ago

heir someone who inherits or is entitled to become the next ruler

immortality ability to live forever

legend story from ancient times that is not always true

mercury silvery-white metal

nobles highest classes in certain societies

offering something that people give as part of a religious ceremony or ritual

peasants uneducated people who are often the lowest rank in society

rebels people who oppose or fight those in power

rituals ceremonies performed for religious reasons

sacrifice animal or human that is killed to honour a god or gods

slaves people who are owned by other people and have to obey them

tribes people who live together, sharing the same language, culture and history

warlords military leaders of a region

Find out more

Books

Ancient China (DK Eyewitness Books), Arthur Cotterell (DK Publishing, 2005)

Ancient China (History Hunters), Louise Spilsbury (Raintree, 2016)

China (Countries Around the World), Patrick Catel (Raintree, 2013)

Daily Life in Shang Dynasty China (Daily Life in Ancient Civilizations), Lori Hile (Raintree, 2016)

The Great Wall of China (Engineering Wonders), Rebecca Stanborough (Raintree, 2016)

Websites

www.bbc.com/bitesize/articles/z2ckrwx
Learn more about the Shang Dynasty.

www.dkfindout.com/uk/history/ancient-china
Find out more about ancient China, and take a quiz to test your knowledge.

www.nationalgeographic.com/archaeology-and-history/archaeology/emperor-qin
Discover more about the Terracotta Army at Emperor Qin's tomb.

Index

afterlife 16, 20, 23, 30, 33
ancestors 22–23, 24, 26
armies 6, 16, 30, 31, 32

battles 4, 5, 7, 16, 27
books 8
burial 8, 9, 16, 17, 19, 20, 25,
    28, 30, 33

chariots 6

dogs 17
dynasties 4–5, 6, 16, 23, 24,
    25, 39, 42, 44
    Han 39, 44
    Shang 4, 5, 16, 23, 24, 25
    Zhou 5, 39, 44

emperors 4, 5, 8–9, 10–11,
    12, 14, 18, 20, 24, 28, 30, 32,
    39, 41, 44
Empress Wu 14–15

feasts 38–39
flaying 12
foot binding 34–35
Forbidden City 11
Fu Hao 16, 17

gods 5, 7, 20, 22, 24, 26, 44
graves 16, 17, 22, 23
Great Wall of China 9

jade 20, 21

kites 7

make-up 34, 36–37
medicines 42–43

oracle bones 26–27

palaces 11, 14, 18, 30, 32

rituals 22, 23, 25, 27

sacrifice 5, 16, 17, 18, 19, 23,
    24–25, 26, 27
silk 28–29, 34, 36
slaves 5, 8, 32–33
spies 12–13

toilets 40–41
tombs 17, 18–19, 30, 31,
    32, 33
torture 10, 12, 13, 29

warriors 6–7
weapons 6–7, 16